THE HISTORY OF FOODS
CONDIMENTS

by Kristine Spanier, MLIS

Ideas for Parents and Teachers

Pogo Books let children practice reading informational text while introducing them to nonfiction features such as headings, labels, sidebars, maps, and diagrams, as well as a table of contents, glossary, and index.

Carefully leveled text with a strong photo match offers early fluent readers the support they need to succeed.

Before Reading

- "Walk" through the book and point out the various nonfiction features. Ask the student what purpose each feature serves.
- Look at the glossary together. Read and discuss the words.

During Reading

- Have the child read the book independently.
- Invite them to list questions that arise from reading.

After Reading

- Discuss the child's questions. Talk about how they might find answers to those questions.
- Prompt the child to think more. Ask: Do you add condiments to any of your foods? Which ones?

Pogo Books are published by Jump!
3500 American Blvd W, Suite 150
Bloomington, MN 55431
www.jumplibrary.com

Copyright © 2026 Jump!
International copyright reserved in all countries.
No part of this book may be reproduced in any form without written permission from the publisher.

Jump! is a division of FlutterBee Education Group.

Library of Congress Cataloging-in-Publication Data

Names: Spanier, Kristine, author.
Title: Condiments / by Kristine Spanier, MLIS.
Description: Minneapolis, MN: Jump!, Inc., [2026]
Series: The history of foods | Includes index.
Audience: Ages 7-10
Identifiers: LCCN 2024054442 (print)
LCCN 2024054443 (ebook)
ISBN 9798892139038 (hardcover)
ISBN 9798892139045 (paperback)
ISBN 9798892139052 (ebook)
Subjects: LCSH: Condiments—History—Juvenile literature. | Food engineers—History—Juvenile literature.
Classification: LCC TX819.A1 S653 2026 (print)
LCC TX819.A1 (ebook)
DDC 664/.5—dc23/eng/20250116
LC record available at https://lccn.loc.gov/2024054442
LC ebook record available at https://lccn.loc.gov/2024054443

Editor: Jenna Gleisner
Designer: Molly Ballanger

Photo Credits: Shutterstock, cover, 3, 20; IDEA ROUTE/Shutterstock, 1; Image Source/iStock, 4; DenisMArt/Shutterstock, 5; Carlos Yudica/Shutterstock, 6-7 (left); Kirill Aleksandrovich/Shutterstock, 6-7 (right); Tanya Sid/Shutterstock, 6-7 (background); Fotoviv/Dreamstime, 8-9; H.J. Heinz Company Photographs, 1864-2001, MSP 57, Detre Library & Archives, Senator John Heinz History Center, 10; MSPhotographic/iStock, 10-11; Pixel-Shot/Shutterstock, 12; adsR/Alamy, 13; Transcendental Graphics/Getty, 14; Paulina Rojas/Shutterstock, 14-15; JHVEPhoto/Shutterstock, 16-17; New Africa/Shutterstock, 18 (left); Julie Clopper/Shutterstock, 18 (right); The Image Party/Shutterstock, 19; Billy F Blume Jr/Shutterstock, 20-21; JeniFoto/Shutterstock, 23.

Printed in the United States of America at Corporate Graphics in North Mankato, Minnesota.

TABLE OF CONTENTS

CHAPTER 1
First Condiments..4

CHAPTER 2
Condiments in the 1900s...........................12

CHAPTER 3
Global Flavors..18

QUICK FACTS & TOOLS
Timeline...22
Glossary...23
Index...24
To Learn More..24

CHAPTER 1
FIRST CONDIMENTS

Do you put ketchup on your fries? Tomato ketchup is a **condiment**. It was **invented** more than 200 years ago! Condiments add **flavor**. They make foods taste better.

ketchup

In 1812, James Mease created a tomato sauce **recipe**. In 1876, H.J. Heinz made his own **version**. The Heinz company now sells more than 650 million bottles of ketchup a year!

CHAPTER 1   5

John Wheeley Lea and William Perrins lived in Worcester, England. In 1837, they created a sauce. It had anchovies. It smelled bad! They put it in the **cellar**. They forgot about it. It **fermented**. A year later, it had turned into a tasty sauce. They named it Worcestershire sauce. Today, people put it on meats.

DID YOU KNOW?

Lea and Perrins shipped their sauce. The bottles were wrapped in paper. This kept them from breaking. The bottles are still wrapped in paper today!

Edmund McIlhenny lived in Louisiana in the 1860s. He thought food there lacked flavor. He had a garden. He grew peppers. He made a spicy sauce with them. He called it Tabasco. It is now sold in more than 195 countries!

WHAT DO YOU THINK?

Tabasco is named after a Mexican state. Why? It is where the peppers to make the sauce were originally grown. What would you name a hot sauce? Why?

The Heinz company made a relish recipe in 1889. It was based on one from India. It had chopped bell peppers and vegetables. They were mixed with spices. Sweet pickle relish is now a top seller!

1904 bottle

10 CHAPTER 1

CHAPTER 1 · 11

CHAPTER 2
CONDIMENTS IN THE 1900s

George and Francis French were brothers. They had a food company. In 1904, they made a yellow mustard. It had mustard seeds, vinegar, and spices.

mustard seeds

At first, they called it Cream Salad Mustard. It was invented as a salad **dressing**. It was creamy. It didn't have a strong taste. The recipe was a hit! People put it on salads. They put it on meats, too.

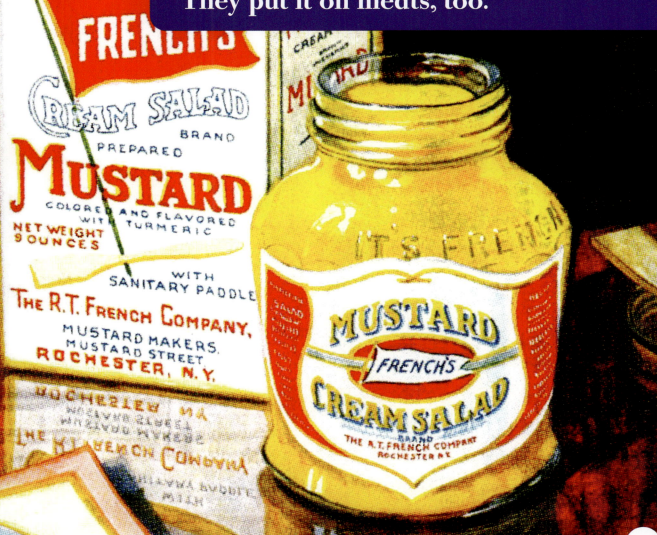

CHAPTER 2

The recipe for mayonnaise came from France. It was made with eggs, oil, and vinegar. At first, people made it at home. They put it on sandwiches.

Richard Hellmann had a **deli** in New York. In 1920, he started selling mayo. Soon, everyone had jars of it in their kitchens.

Do you like ranch dressing? If so, you can thank Steve Henson. In 1949, he invented a dressing. He started with mayo and sour cream. He added herbs and seasonings. People loved it!

In 1954, Henson moved to California. He lived on a ranch. He named the dressing Hidden Valley. He sold packets of it to guests. He couldn't keep up with **demand**!

WHAT DO YOU THINK?

Henson sold his recipe in 1972. He sold it for $8 million. Do you think he should have kept the recipe a secret? Why or why not?

CHAPTER 2　17

CHAPTER 3
GLOBAL FLAVORS

Condiments are created around the world. The first soy sauces were made in China. Soy sauce as we know it comes from Japan. Three families formed a soy sauce company in 1917. It became Kikkoman in 1964. Soy sauce has a salty, meaty flavor.

A spicy sauce is popular in Si Racha, Thailand. In 1980, David Tran started a company in California. He created a similar sauce. He named it after the town. It is called sriracha sauce.

CHAPTER 3 19

TAKE A LOOK!

What countries are some of the most popular condiments from? Take a look!

ENGLAND
Worcestershire sauce

CHINA
soy sauce

FRANCE
mayonnaise

INDIA
relish

UNITED STATES
ranch dressing

THAILAND
sriracha sauce

Store shelves are filled with condiments. What do you like to put on your food? Are you ready to try something new?

CHAPTER 3 21

QUICK FACTS & TOOLS

TIMELINE

Take a look at some important dates in the history of condiments!

1812
James Mease creates tomato ketchup. H.J. Heinz makes a new version 64 years later.

1837
John Wheeley Lea and William Perrins create what becomes Worcestershire sauce.

1904
George and Francis French invent and start selling yellow mustard.

1868
Edmund McIlhenny invents Tabasco sauce.

1889
Heinz introduces India Relish.

1980
David Tran creates sriracha sauce in California.

1920
Richard Hellmann sells his first jars of mayonnaise.

1949
Steve Henson invents ranch dressing. He begins selling it in 1954.

GLOSSARY

cellar: A room below ground level, often used for storage.

condiment: Something, such as a sauce, that is added to food, usually after the food is prepared, to add flavor.

deli: A store that sells prepared foods, such as salads and sliced meats.

demand: Desire to buy or use something.

dressing: A sauce for salads.

fermented: When food or drinks are changed by good bacteria or yeast over time, making them taste different.

flavor: Taste.

invented: Created and produced for the first time.

recipe: Instructions for preparing food, including what ingredients are needed.

version: A different or changed form of something.

QUICK FACTS & TOOLS   23

INDEX

Cream Salad Mustard 13
French, Francis 12
French, George 12
Heinz company 5, 10
Heinz, H.J. 5
Hellmann, Richard 14
Henson, Steve 17
ketchup 4, 5
Kikkoman 18
Lea, John Wheeley 6
mayonnaise 14, 17, 20
McIlhenny, Edmund 9

Mease, James 5
mustard 12, 13
Perrins, William 6
ranch dressing 17, 20
recipe 5, 10, 13, 14, 17
relish 10, 20
sells 5, 9, 10, 14, 17
soy sauces 18, 20
sriracha sauce 19, 20
Tabasco 9
Tran, David 19
Worcestershire sauce 6, 20

TO LEARN MORE

Finding more information is as easy as 1, 2, 3.
1. Go to www.factsurfer.com
2. Enter "condiments" into the search box.
3. Choose your book to see a list of websites.

24   QUICK FACTS & TOOLS